WHAT I KNOW NOW

Yusef Andre Wiley
What I Know Now

Cover design by Olayemi Bolaji

Published by Spines
ISBN: 979-8-89569-982-9

WHAT I KNOW NOW

THE GUIDE TO A GROWTH MINDSET

YUSEF ANDRE WILEY

CONTENTS

KEYNOTE SPEAKER BIO

Yusef Andre Wiley is a seasoned keynote speaker with over 25 years of experience captivating audiences worldwide. His profound insights and engaging delivery have transformed the lives of hundreds, earning him a reputation as a dynamic influencer and thought leader in personal development and social change.

Throughout his illustrious career, Yusef Andre Wiley has leveraged his expertise to build a successful multimillion-dollar organization dedicated to empowering individuals to overcome adversity and realize their full potential. His unwavering commitment to social impact has seen him collaborate with numerous nonprofit leaders, igniting change and fostering sustainable growth in communities across the globe.

As a distinguished member of the John Maxwell Team and TEDx speaker, Yusef Andre Wiley has shared his expertise on prestigious platforms, inspiring countless individuals to embrace change and pursue excellence. His thought-provoking presentations are enriched by his diverse experiences and deep-rooted passion for driving positive change.

Yusef Andre Wiley's impact extends beyond the stage, as he has spearheaded multiple successful reentry programs aimed at supporting justice-involved individuals in their transition to society. His unparalleled dedication to helping others has resulted in hundreds of formerly incarcerated individuals securing viable employment opportunities, fostering a sense of hope and empowerment in marginalized communities.

Recognized as a leading consultant in his field, Yusef Andre Wiley has been sought after by startup organizations seeking to make a meaningful difference in the world. His strategic guidance and subject matter expertise have been instrumental in shaping the success of numerous initiatives, setting the stage for sustainable growth and impact.

With a rare blend of authenticity, expertise, and empathy, Yusef Andre Wiley continues to inspire audiences to embrace change, unlock their potential, and make a lasting difference in the world. His transformative messages resonate deeply with audiences of all backgrounds, leaving a lasting impression and sparking meaningful action.

In booking Yusef Andre Wiley as your keynote speaker, you're not just securing a speaker; you're investing in a transformative experience that will empower your audience to reach new heights of personal and professional growth.

TOP TEN KEYNOTES

1. “From Punishment to Rehabilitation: Rethinking Approaches to Criminal Justice"
2. "Breaking the Cycle: Strategies for Successful Reentry and Rehabilitation"
3. "Beyond Bars: Transforming Lives Through Alternative Sentencing Programs"
4. "The Role of Community Engagement in Criminal Justice Reform"
5. "Injustice in Black and White: Addressing Racial Disparities in the Criminal Justice System"
6. "From Cells to Success: Empowering Formerly Incarcerated Individuals in the Workforce"
7. "Restorative Justice: Healing Communities and Restoring Trust"
8. "The Intersection of Mental Health and the Criminal Justice System"

9. "Challenging the School-to-Prison Pipeline: Creating Pathways for Youth Success"
10. "Policy Matters: Advocating for Legislative Change in Criminal Justice Reform"

Each of these topics offers a unique perspective on criminal justice reform, addressing various aspects of the system and providing insights into potential solutions and strategies for improvement.

PREFACE

"What I Know Now" serves as the poignant sequel to the autobiography "If I Knew Then," delving deeper into the realities of change and adaptation post-incarceration. This book sheds light on the complexities of transitioning to a life of freedom and responsibility, embodying the essence of living out that change with integrity and resilience. Unlike conventional biographies, "What I Know Now" serves as a practical, step-by-step guide for individuals navigating the challenges of reintegration into society, drawing from the experiences and wisdom of Yusef Wiley, a formerly incarcerated individual turned advocate for positive change.

One of the primary challenges faced by individuals upon reentering society after incarceration is the stigma and barriers associated with a criminal record. From finding stable employment to rebuilding relationships and establishing a sense of community, the journey to becoming an upstanding citizen can be fraught with obstacles and setbacks. Additionally, navigating the complexities of daily life without the structure and support of the prison environment can pose significant challenges, requiring a strong sense of self-discipline and determination.

However, amidst these challenges lies the greatest reward of all – the opportunity to embrace true transformation and become a changed person. The sense of liberation that comes with breaking free from the confines of a troubled past and embracing a future filled with hope and purpose is unparalleled. The ability to live authentically, in alignment with one's values and principles, is a testament to the resilience and strength of the human spirit. The greatest gift of being a changed person lies in the ability to inspire others, to share one's journey of growth and redemption, and to offer guidance and support to those embarking on a similar path of self-discovery and renewal. "What I Know Now" serves as a beacon of hope and guidance for individuals seeking to navigate the complexities of change and transformation post-incarceration, illuminating the profound impact of personal growth and resilience in the face of adversity.

GETTING OUT WITH LOTS OF LOVE

The data for African Americans re-entering society after incarceration reveals several challenging statistics. While specific figures can vary over time and by source, some key points generally include:

1. Recidivism Rates: African Americans often face higher recidivism rates compared to other demographic groups. Studies indicate that around 60-70% of released inmates may return to prison within three years.

2. Employment Challenges: Many formerly incarcerated individuals struggle to find stable employment due to stigma and legal barriers, which can be particularly pronounced for African Americans.

3. Housing Instability: Access to affordable housing can be a significant issue, with many facing discrimination or difficulties securing housing due to their criminal records.

4. Health Disparities: Released individuals often have unmet health needs, including mental health and substance abuse issues, which can be exacerbated by prior incarceration experiences.

5. Support Systems: The availability of community support programs can vary widely, impacting the reintegration process for African Americans.

These issues underscore the systemic challenges faced by many African Americans upon re-entry into society after incarceration.

In my case, on May 24, 2012, I was received by a loving community with open arms which set the stage for my journey to defy these staggering odds. My finance and now wife Sanae, my mother and father, my sister Donna and my teacher and mentor Shaykh Rami Nsour and his mother and the rest of the Nsour family ensured that I was set up for success. But is this the case for the average person getting out of prison? No! absolutely not. Building trust with community and family members is going to be a challenge, and if you burn a lot of bridges with folks, it is going to be that much harder to win them over again. Setting goals and having a written plan has been part of my anchor towards building a successful career in the nonprofit and for-profit world. Getting there is challenging and for me getting my first job at Tayba Foundation was the most rewarding situation because my teacher and mentor allowed me to the time to grow into the role of operations manager while on the side allowing me to build my dream of the Timelist Group, Inc. I will admit, it was hard to stay focused at times on Tayba because I was so driven to build my dream, however, this great start also landed me in my second job at Averroes High School in Fremont California as the Islamic Studies teacher for High School students. Without the referral from Shaykh Rami, I would not have even gotten this opportunity which also resulted in me being able to move my family to the Bay Area from Southern California. At the time, Imam Tahir and Ustadh Usama Canon sat on the Board of Averroes and they approved my hire. And guess what, I was still wearing an ankle monitor from parole serving as a school teacher. Getting out with lots of love creates the momentum to reach great heights, but you cannot slow down one bit, you cannot become complacent or content with the basics or else the world will past you up very quickly and it will feel as though you must start over again in an ecosystem that doesn't favor people with felony backgrounds. So, please remember these 5 things:

1. Set goals
2. Write out a plan of action
3. Stay focused, don't give up no matter what
4. Maintain employment while you build your career on the side
5. Keep going and never become complacent

COMING HOME TO EXPECTATIONS

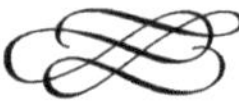

Most people encounter problems with others due to unmet expectations for several reasons:

1. Communication Gaps: Misunderstandings often arise when expectations are not clearly communicated. Assumptions about what others know or believe can lead to conflicts.

2. Differing Perspectives: People have unique backgrounds, values, and experiences, which shape their expectations. When these differ significantly, it can lead to friction.

3. Unrealistic Expectations: Sometimes, individuals set expectations that are too high or unrealistic, leading to disappointment and frustration when others fail to meet them.

4. Fear of Vulnerability: People may hesitate to express their needs or expectations, resulting in unvoiced grievances that can build resentment over time.

5. Cultural Differences: Cultural backgrounds can influence how expectations are formed and communicated, leading to potential misunderstandings in diverse settings.

6. Change Over Time: Expectations can evolve, and if parties do not adapt to these changes, it can create conflict.

Being aware of these factors and fostering open communication can help mitigate issues related to expectations in relationships.

As the years rolled by in the vibrant yet challenging Bay Area, I found myself grappling with the realities of family responsibilities and the pressing need for independence. The bustling life around me, filled with diverse cultures and communities, painted a beautiful picture, but beneath it lay a struggle that was becoming increasingly difficult to manage. My circle of friends was a rich tapestry of cultures: Pakistanis, Arabs, Indians, Yemenis, Afghanis, and a close-knit group of African Americans from the Lighthouse Mosque community. Each relationship brought its own set of expectations and dynamics, and I soon found myself at the intersection of these two worlds.

What struck me was the contrasting roles I played within these communities. In the African American community, I had established myself as a leader and teacher, someone they looked up to for guidance. Yet, to my surprise, it was my Southeast Asian friends who sought mentorship from me, eager for insights on how to steer their children away from the pitfalls of gangs and substance abuse. This unexpected demand created an intriguing dynamic. I had anticipated my African American peers would be the ones turning to me for support, but it was the Southeast

Asian families who actively sought my help. Thankfully, they were willing to pay for my mentoring services; without that income, surviving the high cost of living in the Bay Area on a teacher's salary would have been nearly impossible.

In fact, the only reason I managed to stay in the Bay Area for four and a half years was due to a combination of consulting work, mentoring, and my position at Averroes High School. Each day was a balancing act, as I juggled these commitments while trying to provide for my family. My journey took a pivotal turn when one of my mentors and a board member of Timelist approached me with an idea that would change everything. He suggested that it was time for me to commit to Timelist full-time and offered to help me raise the necessary capital to realize my nonprofit dream. It was an exciting prospect, yet it also added to the weight of my responsibilities.

One day, while driving along the 580 freeway from Richmond to Union City, the weight of my circumstances felt particularly heavy. The soaring cost of living in the Bay Area loomed large in my mind, and I couldn't shake the feeling of being overwhelmed. In that moment, I picked up the phone and called my wife, Sanae. “Hey babe,” I said, my voice tinged with uncertainty, “are you ready to go back home?” Her response was immediate: “SoCal?” I nodded, even though she couldn't see me. “Yes!” In that instant, we made the momentous decision to leave the Bay Area together.

It was a bittersweet moment for me. Leaving meant stepping away from a community I had invested so much in, from friendships that had blossomed and relationships that had deepened over time. While I was excited about the prospect of a new beginning in Southern California, I couldn't help but feel a pang of sadness at the thought of saying goodbye to so many people who had become like family.

As I began to search for a new place to live in SoCal, I was simultaneously exploring every possible avenue to stay in the Bay Area. I even took a second job at Rubicon Programs, hoping to extend my stay. I reached out to the Muslims in the South Bay, believing that my growing mentoring network there could lead to new job opportunities and a larger home for my family. At that time, we were cramped in an 800-square-foot two-bedroom apartment with a single bathroom, and our rent had skyrocketed from $1,475 in 2012 to an eye-watering $2,150 by 2016. The pressure was mounting, and the need for a change was undeniable.

Through it all, I realized that my journey was about much more than just finding a job or a place to live; it was about carving out a future for my family and maintaining the connections that meant so much to me. As I navigated these transitions, I held onto the hope that my efforts would lead to a better life, not just for myself but for the many young lives I sought to impact through mentoring and support.

THE STRUGGLE IS REAL

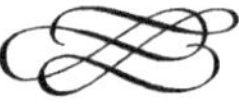

The following was taken from an original email that I sent out to my community for help to sustain my operations in the Bay Area.

Mar 26, 2016, 1:52 PM

As salaamu alaykum dear friend and brother in Islam,

I hope and pray that you and your family are well. Once again, I am reaching out to you seeking your support in advancing our program way beyond myself and after I'm gone. We need your investment into this program as it gains more and more traction in the general community. We received endorsement and regular contributions now from Fremont Unitarian Congregation Church and the South Bay Community Church led by Pastor Bryan Murphy.

Today, I am asking for a monthly commitment of $10.00-$75.00. Being a recurring donor benefits us more now as we have rolled out our new set of programs (see below). Your support will be much appreciated, and we look forward to the opportunity to be a continuous service to the underserved.

Monday - Thursday	10:00 – 3:00 pm	Intake/Screening	Continuous	Cohort
Monday	4:00 – 7:00 pm	Life Skills to Employment	6 – 8 wks.	10-15
Tuesday	4:00 – 7:00 pm	Life Skills to Employment	“ “	“ “
Wednesday	4:00 – 7:00 pm	Life Skills to Employment	“ “	“ “
Monday - Thursday	10:00 – 3:00 pm	Job Readiness and Placement	Landscaping, janitorial or construction	5-10
Monday	3:00 – 6:00 pm	Career Pathway course 1	8 – 12 wks.	5-10
Tuesday	3:00 – 6:00 pm	Career Pathway course 2	“ “	“ “
Wednesday	3:00 – 6:00 pm	Career Pathway course 3	“ “	“ “

JOBS TO CAREERS

http://timelistgroup.org/sponsor

A) 6-8 Week course - soft skills, life skills training and leadership development: Graduation Certificate

B) Landscaping, Janitorial, Construction program: $13-$15 an hour

C) 8-12 Week Career Pathway course options – CompTIA, IT essentials, nursing and other certification programs: weekly monetary stipend

Partners: Timelist Group, SBCC-Genesis, New Haven Adult School, Roots Community Clinic, Tri-City One Stop Career Center, Ohlone College and Youth and Family Services.

Intake Site: TimeList Group, 328 Decoto Road, Suite 124 Union City CA 94587. Tel: 510.431.3606 Fax: 510.431.3582 email: info@timelistgroup.org

Bro. Yusef-Andre Wiley

Andre L. Wiley Sr.

Executive Director

Timelist Group

Mailing: P.O. Box 59009 Los Angeles, CA 90059

-OR- P.O. Box 735 Hayward, CA 94543

Office: 1328 Decoto Rd. Suite 124 Union City, CA 94587

Tel: (510) 431-3606 | Fax: (510) 431-3582 || www.timelist-group.org

The journey to establish a new life in Southern California had its share of challenges, but finally, a ray of hope appeared on the horizon. After countless searches and disappointments, I stumbled upon a rental home in Lancaster that felt like a dream come true. It was a spacious four-bedroom, two-bathroom house, and at just $1,800 a month, it was significantly more affordable than the sky-high rents I had encountered in the Bay Area. My heart raced with excitement; this was a place where my family could truly thrive. However, my enthusiasm was tempered by the reality that I needed double the rent upfront to move in—an obstacle that seemed daunting.

In that moment, I turned to my faith community for support. Their willingness to help me secure this new beginning was both humbling and heartwarming. It reminded me that I was not alone in this fight for a better life. I had missed out on 22 years of opportunities—22 years of building a career, 22 years of educational pursuits, and 22 years of saving for the future with 401(k) plans and IRAs. This transition from the Bay Area reignited a fierce determination within me. I knew I had to hustle harder, not just for myself, but for my family's future.

With my belongings loaded into a U-Haul truck, I made one last stop at my parole office to ensure my paperwork for the transfer to Southern California was in order. Hours slipped by as I anxiously waited. My wife, Sanae, urged me to let her go ahead, but I insisted she stay with me. Finally, the clerk called my name, and I felt a surge of relief as they confirmed that my paperwork was cleared. We were ready to embark on this new chapter.

Upon arriving in Lancaster, I called my two older sons, AJ and Andrew, to help unload the truck. They had been estranged for some time, and I saw this as an opportunity to bridge the gap between them. Surprisingly, the plan worked—at least for about 24 hours. The act of working together, hauling boxes and furniture, provided a brief respite from their tensions.

As dawn broke on my first day in our new home, I received a phone call from my parole officer in Oakland. My heart sank as I listened to the words: I was not cleared to stay in Southern

California and had 24 hours to return to Oakland or face a violation of my parole. Panic surged through me, and my mind raced. I jumped out of bed, threw on some clothes, and hopped into my car, speeding down the 5 Freeway back to the Bay Area.

The drive felt interminable, each mile stretching out the anxiety that gripped me. I arrived at the parole office, my heart pounding in my chest. The officer in front of me appeared focused on her computer, her fingers typing quickly. She paused several times, and my stomach twisted with apprehension. Finally, she looked up and said, "My mistake—the system just took a little while to update. You're free to go back home to SoCal."

Relief washed over me like a wave, but I couldn't help but think about the gas money I had just wasted on that unnecessary five-hour drive. The struggle was undeniably real, but I took a deep breath and reminded myself: once I was off parole, there would be no looking back. This was my chance to build a new life for my family, to seize the opportunities that had eluded me for so long.

As I drove back to Lancaster, I felt a renewed sense of purpose. The road ahead was filled with uncertainty, but I was determined to face it with courage and resilience. I envisioned a future where I could create stability for my loved ones, a future free from the shadows of my past. Each challenge strengthened my resolve, and I knew that this time, I would fight harder than ever to secure the life we deserved. Our new home in Lancaster would not just be a house; it would be a foundation upon which we could rebuild, grow, and flourish together.

Now that I'm back home—though not quite in the bustling city of Los Angeles, but close enough—I find myself on a mission to forge new connections. My focus is on organizations dedicated to serving the reentry population and the Muslim community, as I seek to establish a faith-based home that resonates with my values and aspirations.

Upon my return, it quickly became evident that Southern California is a stark contrast to the vibrant community I had experienced in the Bay Area. In the Bay, I was enveloped in a warm embrace of support from the Tayba family and the unified spirit of the Bay Area Muslims. There, love and camaraderie flourished, creating a nurturing environment where collaboration thrived. However, in Los Angeles, the landscape feels vastly different. The city is enormous and sprawling, lacking the close-knit culture I had grown accustomed to. People here often seem more guarded and suspicious, leading to a palpable sense of competition for limited resources. I witnessed individuals squabbling over funding crumbs, and it became clear that the friendliness I once knew was not as prevalent.

Initially, I felt disheartened and contemplated returning to the Bay Area, where the sense of community was strong and supportive. Just when I was on the verge of giving up, I had the fortunate opportunity to meet Janie Hodges from the Paving the Way Foundation. She stood out as a beacon of hope in Lancaster, being one of the few individuals actively engaged in reentry work. Her genuine kindness and openness provided a refreshing contrast to the environment I had encountered thus far.

During our conversation, Janie shared stories of numerous individuals who had moved to Lancaster only to feel overwhelmed and ultimately leave. She encouraged me not to follow in their footsteps, emphasizing that the community needed passionate and dedicated people like me. Her words resonated deeply within me, igniting a renewed sense of purpose. From that moment on, I made a commitment to help build up Lancaster and the greater LA County area through our model reentry program.

I envision creating a supportive network that not only aids those reentering society but also fosters a sense of belonging and unity among the Muslim community. By leveraging my experiences and the insights gained from inspiring individuals like Janie, I hope to bridge the gaps I've encountered and cultivate a thriving community where everyone can flourish together. My mission is clear: to transform Lancaster into a place where faith, support, and collaboration are at the forefront, ensuring that no one feels alone in their journey.

I knew that I would need to do a lot of grnding and research to figure out how I could make it work living in Lancaster California where I knew resources would be limited. I also knew that I would still need to replant roots back in the city of LA. But what I learned about doing business as a 501(c)(3) is that nonprofits in smaller communities often face unique challenges that make their operations more difficult compared to those in larger cities like Los Angeles. Here are several key reasons for this struggle:

1. Limited Resources: Smaller communities typically have fewer financial resources. Donors may be less abundant, and the competition for funding can be intense, especially when larger organizations with established networks are also vying for the same grants and donations. This can lead to a scarcity of funds for essential programs and services.

2. Reduced Visibility: Nonprofits in smaller communities often lack the visibility that larger organizations in major cities enjoy. Without media coverage, robust marketing strategies, or a strong online presence, these organizations can struggle to attract attention and build a supporter base.

3. Less Diverse Funding Opportunities: Larger cities tend to have a wider range of funding sources, including private foundations, corporate sponsorships, and government grants. In contrast, smaller communities may have limited local foundations and fewer corporations willing to invest in community initiatives, making it harder for nonprofits to secure diverse funding lines.

4. Community Size and Connections: In smaller towns, the community is often tightly knit. While this can foster strong relationships, it can also limit outreach and engagement with individuals who may not be part of the existing network. Nonprofits may struggle to connect with new constituents or supporters outside their immediate circles.

5. Staffing Challenges: Nonprofits in smaller areas may find it difficult to recruit and retain qualified staff. There may be fewer professionals with the necessary skills or experience, and

salaries might not be competitive with those offered in larger cities. This can lead to high turnover rates and a lack of continuity in programs.

6. Limited Program Offerings: In smaller communities, the demand for specific services may not be as high, which can lead to fewer program offerings. Nonprofits may struggle to tailor their services to meet community needs effectively, resulting in underutilized programs.

7. Volunteer Base: While many nonprofits rely on volunteers, smaller communities may have a limited pool of individuals who can volunteer their time. Competing commitments, such as work and family obligations, can further restrict the availability of potential volunteers.

8. Economic Challenges: Smaller communities may face economic hardships that impact the overall well-being of their residents. High unemployment rates and lower income levels can affect the community's ability to support local nonprofits, both through donations and volunteerism.

9. Social Dynamics: In some smaller communities, social dynamics can create barriers to collaboration. Nonprofits may face challenges when trying to work together due to competition for limited resources or differing priorities within the community.

10. Infrastructure and Support: Larger cities often have established networks and support systems for nonprofits, including training, mentorship, and collaboration opportunities. Smaller

communities might lack these supportive infrastructures, making it harder for nonprofits to grow and innovate.

In summary, while nonprofits in smaller communities play a vital role in addressing local needs, they face significant challenges that can hinder their effectiveness and sustainability. Addressing these issues requires innovative solutions and increased support from local governments, foundations, and the broader community. Finding this in Lancaster would indeed be a challenge as I learned very quickly that there was a good-ole boy network in town that had its very few chosen organizations that they would support who have become the gatekeeper of nonprofit activities in the Lancaster Antelope Valley community.

The one thing about me though is that I've always found a way to connect with people of all types, it is about the mission, not the personality of folks. We must learn how to get past our own egos if we intend to serve a greater cause and purpose. A few good-ole boys are not going to stop me or the mission of the Timelist Group, Inc. Keep up the prayers, stay focus and believe in the resolve of the human spirit.

THE BROTHERHOOD

"The likeness of the believers in their love and compassion is that of a body; if a limb of it is afflicted, the entirety responds with fever and sleeplessness". Prophet Muhammad (Peace Be Upon Him).

Having a faith community, whether it be a brotherhood or sisterhood in Islam or Christianity, offers numerous inherent benefits:

1. Support System: Members provide emotional and spiritual support to one another during difficult times, fostering a sense of belonging and security.

2. Shared Values and Beliefs: Being part of a faith community reinforces shared values and ethical principles, helping individuals navigate life's challenges with a moral compass.

3. Encouragement in Faith: Regular gatherings and activities encourage members to deepen their faith practices, such as prayer, worship, and community service.

4. Social Connections: Faith communities often foster friendships and social networks, reducing feelings of isolation and loneliness.

5. Opportunities for Service: Many faith communities engage in charitable activities, providing members with opportunities to serve others and contribute positively to society.

6. Cultural and Spiritual Education: These communities often emphasize learning about religious texts, traditions, and practices, enhancing members' understanding and appreciation of their faith.

7. Rituals and Celebrations: Sharing in rituals, holidays, and ceremonies strengthens bonds among members and creates a sense of continuity and tradition.

8. Accountability: Being part of a community encourages personal accountability in one's faith journey, helping individuals stay committed to their beliefs and values.

9. Diversity and Perspective: Engaging with a diverse group within the faith community can provide new perspectives and insights, enriching personal growth and understanding.

10. Mental Well-being: Participation in a faith community has been linked to improved mental health, as it can reduce stress and anxiety through communal support and shared practices.

Overall, faith communities foster a sense of unity, purpose, and belonging, which can be profoundly transformative for individuals. So, for me, it was ISLAH LA where I found this unity and the sense of belonging and a great leadership in Imam Jihad Saafir. When Imam Jihad learned that I was leading a nonprofit that focused on justice involved individuals, he immediately jumped in with no strings attached to support our efforts by opening up the Food Pantry services to us and giving us the platform to share our message to the Islah LA community. This is what we call the Brotherhood

BECOMING MY TRUE SELF

It is May 2017, a pivotal month that stands as a significant milestone in my life. During this time, I found myself making frequent trips back and forth to the Bay Area, reconnecting with my faith roots, my tech friends, and the vibrant community that had shaped my early years. Each journey was not just a mere visit; it was a pilgrimage of sorts, laden with emotion and the weight of my past experiences.

On this particular occasion, I was filled with anticipation as I reached out to my parole officer to request a travel pass. The destination was Zaytuna College, where I was set to attend an evening event featuring some of the most revered scholars and leaders in my life: Shaykh Hamza Yusuf, Imam Tahir, Shaykh Abdullah Hamid Ali, and Imam Zaid Shakir. These figures had not only influenced my understanding of faith but had also served as guiding lights during the tumultuous years prior to my release from prison. The prospect of being in the same room as these intellectual giants was exhilarating, and I was eager to soak in their wisdom and insights.

However, as the days ticked down, a sense of unease began to creep in. My attempts to reach my parole officer were met with silence. Text messages remained unanswered, and phone calls went straight to voicemail. I couldn't shake the feeling that something was amiss. The clock was ticking, and the event was fast approaching. Would I be able to attend, or would this be yet another opportunity snatched away from me?

Just when despair was starting to settle in, I received a call the day before my trip. It was around 9:00 AM when my phone buzzed, and I saw my parole officer's name flashing on the screen. My heart raced as I answered, hopeful yet apprehensive. To my utter disbelief, he informed me that he had seen my requests but that I no longer needed a travel pass—because I was off parole! The weight of his words hit me like a tidal wave. I was no longer bound by the restrictions that had defined my existence for so long.

In that moment, I felt an exhilarating rush of freedom that was almost overwhelming. My wife was nearby when I received the news, and in my sheer joy, I nearly bumped my head on the ceiling of our home as I jumped with excitement. The realization that I was free to pursue my passions without the constraints of parole was liberating. I could hardly contain my excitement, and I shared the news with my wife, who quickly got dressed and headed out for lunch, giving me space to process this monumental shift in my life.

This was not just a personal victory; it symbolized a new chapter filled with endless possibilities. With the proverbial gloves now off, I felt an invigoration coursing through my veins. The grind that lay ahead was no longer a burden but a thrilling challenge. I was ready to shift into overdrive, to push myself beyond the limits I had previously accepted. The journey from incarceration to liberation was not just about physical freedom; it was about seizing every opportunity to grow, learn, and contribute to my community.

As I prepared for my trip to the Bay Area, I reflected on the road that had led me here. The struggles, the setbacks, and the lessons learned in prison had all played a crucial role in shaping my perspective. I had spent countless nights contemplating my future, my purpose, and the legacy I wanted to leave behind. Now, with the shackles of my past finally cast aside, I felt a renewed sense of purpose and direction.

Attending the event at Zaytuna College was more than just an opportunity to hear from esteemed scholars; it was a chance to immerse myself in a community of like-minded individuals who shared a commitment to knowledge and personal growth. I envisioned the conversations I would engage in, the friendships I would rekindle, and the inspiration I would draw from those around me. Each moment spent in the company of such influential figures would serve as a reminder of the importance of mentorship and the power of education in transforming lives.

As I set out for the Bay Area, I carried with me a sense of hope and determination. The journey ahead was not just about attending an event; it was about embracing my newfound freedom and the opportunities it presented. I was ready to step into this new chapter with open arms, fueled by the wisdom of the past and the promise of the future. This was my moment, and I was determined to make the most of it. Becoming my true self has begun without the barriers from the California Department of Corrections and Rehabilitation.

In my journey to facilitate housing programs for individuals reentering society, many of my trips revolved around hosting workshops aimed at discussing how the Bay Area could implement similar initiatives to those I had successfully established in Southern California. This section of my book: Becoming My True Self' outlines a comprehensive framework for creating effective housing programs, divided into three distinct phases. Phase 1 focuses on foundational agreements and documentation, phase 2 emphasizes site preparation and operational planning, and phase 3 covers the implementation of housing services.

Phase One: Establishing Foundations

1. Contractual Documents

The initial step in any housing program is to ensure that all necessary contractual documents are prepared for filing and signatures with state and county agencies.

Key Actions.

Identify Partners: Determine potential partners who will collaborate in this initiative.

- Memorandum of Understanding (MOU)**: Establish an MOU between relevant organizations to outline shared responsibilities. This may include agreements for delivering external services at the housing facility, which can be detailed later.

2. Curriculum Development

A structured daily program is essential for the success of the housing initiative. The curriculum should address mealtimes, group activities, and other daily schedules.

Key Actions.

- Create a calendar that includes all program activities, which will be part of the housing documentation submitted to authorities.

3. Staffing

Clearly define roles within the staff and establish specific compensation for each position. Key roles may include:

- Housing Navigator

- House Manager

- Drug and Alcohol Counselor

4. Funding Sources

Explore various funding avenues to support the program, including:

- Request for Proposals (RFPs)

- Grant writer

- Housing contracts

- Fundraising initiatives

5. Site Identification

Identify a suitable location for the housing facility. Considerations include:

- Location suitability and reasons for selection

- Verification of property ownership by the leasing agent, including proof of ownership or lease agreement to be attached to the contract documents.

6. Target Population

Define the target demographic for the housing program, which may include:

- Parolees

- Probationers

- Individuals with mental health challenges

- Men or women

- Transitional Age Youth

7. Scope of Work

Determine the services that will be offered on-site, such as:

- Medi-Cal enrollment

- Food Stamp services

8. Insurance Requirements

Ensure all necessary insurance policies are in place, including:

- General Commercial Liability Insurance, designating the facility and contractual partners as insured parties.

- Professional Liability Insurance

- Worker's Compensation Insurance

9. Local Business Licenses

Secure any required local business licenses from the county or city.

10. Budget Planning

Develop a preliminary budget to outline expected costs and funding needs.

Phase Two: Site Preparation and Development

Once the foundational agreements are established, the next steps involve preparing the site for operations.

Key Actions.

1. Legal Compliance

Confirm the legality of securing the housing location, including ownership verification, zoning letters, and use permits.

2. Lease Agreement

-Pay the deposit and sign a lease that specifies the property's use for transitional or sober living housing.

Preparations for Operations:

3. Facility Setup

-Prepare the facility for operations by installing necessary safety features (e.g., emergency exit signs and fire extinguishers) and furnishing the space with adequate beds, desks, internet access, and recreational areas.

4. Employee Handbook

-Create an on-site employee handbook detailing policies and procedures.

5. Grievance Policy

-Develop and post a grievance policy for residents.

6. House Rules

-Establish and display house rules for all residents.

7. Orientation Packet

-Prepare an orientation packet that outlines guidelines for residents, including curfews, passes, smoking policies, and loitering rules.

8. Daily Schedule

-Create a comprehensive schedule for day-to-day activities, facilitated by staff or partner organizations.

9. Food Bank Services

-Collaborate with partner organizations to establish food bank services.

10. Staff Conduct Policy

-Develop a staff conduct policy and orientation manual for on-site use.

11. Budget Review

-Finalize the budget for this phase.

Phase Three: Implementation and Operations

With the site prepared, the final phase focuses on implementation and opening the housing facility.

Key Actions.

1. Payroll System (Paycom, ADP, Paylocity, Rippling etc.)

Establish or implement a payroll system for employees.

2. Staffing

-Recruit experienced staff, including a live-in house manager with credentials in alcohol and drug counseling, a house supervisor, mentors, and career coaches who have previously been incarcerated.

3. Employee Handbook

-Finalize the employee handbook for staff reference.

4. Uniform Policy

-Ensure all staff wear identifiable uniforms, such as polo shirts and slacks, to facilitate recognition during house visits by parole or probation officers.

5. Application Review

-Implement a process for reviewing

In this book I'm just scratching the surface of what my workshops look like and how I was able to introduce our model reentry housing program to my immediate community. Because I have been very successful setting up housing programs in southern California, more people are paying attention to me, even in other states and in other countries like Australia and Canada, just to name a few. Free from parole restrictions, it is now time for me to get my passport and other credentials to become more of my true self. Being that Public Speaking and Facilitation had become so important in my life I decided to enroll in the John Maxwell Team program. This was a self-paced program which eventually got me to Orlando Florida for the big live event and graduation in August of 2018. This experience felt more like a celebration of life, next level networking and living my full life. Skies, no limitations.

This trip also gave me an opportunity to take my family to Walt Disney World. This was especially amazing for me to be able to take this trip with my son Amir.

I couldn't contain my excitement as I returned to Lancaster to embark on the thrilling journey of signing my escrow documents for my very first home! This moment marked a significant milestone in my life, and the anticipation of becoming a proud homeowner filled me with a sense of accomplishment and joy. The air was electric with possibility, and I could already envision the countless memories waiting to be made in my new space!

Food for Thought. The chances of an ex-felon buying a home after getting out of prison can vary based on several factors, including:

1. Credit History: Many lenders consider credit history when approving loans. If the ex-felon has managed to rebuild their credit score, they may have better chances of securing a mortgage.

2. Employment Status: Having stable employment can improve an ex-felon's chances, as it demonstrates financial stability and the ability to make regular payments.

3. Down Payment: The ability to provide a substantial down payment can increase the likelihood of approval, as it reduces the lender's risk.

4. State Laws: Some states have laws that can impact an ex-felon's ability to obtain housing, including specific rights regarding discrimination based on criminal history.

5. Lender Policies: Different lenders have varying policies regarding ex-felons. Some may be more lenient than others.

6. Support Programs: There are organizations and programs designed to assist ex-felons in home buying, which can provide resources and guidance.

Overall, while challenges exist, many ex-felons successfully transition to homeownership by addressing these factors. What are you doing to ensure that you or someone that you know will soon be released from prison and needs the help and knowledge to be victorious in his or her reintegration back into the community?

Remember, set goals, write the plan, stay focused, don't become complacent.

IT'S NOT EASY HELPING PEOPLE

As I continue to build the Timelist Group, Inc., we are now on the path to becoming a county operator or provider within one of the biggest Counties in the United States. That big break came with the exchange of the following emails:

On Fri, May 10, 2019, at 5:51 PM < Dr. Kristen Ochoa> wrote:

Hi Yusef,
We are very interested in working with you as an ODR Housing provider, with Timelist as the housing operator.
Are you able to talk on the phone on Tuesday morning, 5/14/19? Let me know what time works for you and Jose and I can jump on the phone with you to talk about the next steps.
We can let you know the outlines of a typical staffing plan, then

loop in our partners at Housing for Health. Though we envision you would get some St. Joseph's ICMS clients at the site, our need right now is for a general ODR Housing site, so clients may have a variety of ODR Housing ICMS providers.
Thanks so much.

-Kristen

Medical Director

Office of Diversion and Reentry

Los Angeles County Department of Health Services

Associate Clinical Professor

David Geffen School of Medicine at UCLA

www.lacounty.gov/diversion

From: Yusef-Andre Wiley <yusefandre@timelistgroup.org>

Sent: Friday, May 10, 2019 3:10 PM

Subject: Re: Potential new beds and programming for ODR participants

Good afternoon all,
I just wanted to follow up on possible opportunities for housing and/or other supportive services through ODR, like case management work through DHS contracting. We recently

received our executed contract for a Master's Agreement for supportive services and housing through LA County. This is a time sensitive issue as we have a 21 bed property and access to a facility for case management for which I need to make a decision on maintain our lease agreement. So, any help would be greatly appreciated on this matter of contracting with ODR, we are very eager, willing and able to get a jump start on this new possible opportunity.
Thank you all again and please enjoy the rest of your day and weekend.
best,

Yusef Wiley

Yusef-Andre Wiley

Timelist Group, Inc

Founder | CEO

3894 Crenshaw Blvd., 8824, Los Angeles CA 90008

2010 W Avenue K #135 Lancaster, CA 93536

Office: (661) 579-0881 | Direct: (510) 552-1256

Timelist|| YouTube || Facebook || Twitter

The email that emerged from our discussions transformed the trajectory of the Timelist Group, solidifying its reputation as a successful nonprofit organization dedicated to addressing critical social issues. This pivotal moment can be traced back to my participation in a panel focused on the homelessness crisis in Los Angeles, an event that highlighted the significant overlap between the homeless population and individuals involved in the justice system.

During the panel, I delivered a presentation that resonated deeply with the audience, sparking conversations about the systemic challenges faced by both communities. My insights shed light on the complex interplay of factors contributing to homelessness and recidivism, including lack of access to resources, mental health issues, and the effects of societal stigma. The engagement from attendees was palpable, with many expressing their appreciation for the nuanced perspective I presented.

Among the panelists was Dr. Kristen, a respected figure in the field, who not only contributed his expertise but also provided a unique lens through which to view the interconnectedness of these two pressing issues. Our discussions after the event further highlighted the potential for collaboration and innovative solutions that could arise from a deeper understanding of both communities' needs.

It was in this context that the game-changing email was drafted. The email encapsulated our shared vision for a more integrated approach to addressing homelessness and justice involvement. It proposed the establishment of initiatives that would leverage our combined resources and expertise to create sustainable support systems for those affected. By fostering partnerships with local organizations, policymakers, and community leaders, we aimed to dismantle the barriers that perpetuate cycles of poverty and incarceration.

The response to this email was overwhelmingly positive, leading to the mobilization of resources and support that had previously been unimaginable. This marked a turning point for the Timelist Group, as we transitioned from a nascent organization to a key player in advocacy and support for marginalized communities. The impact of that initial panel discussion and the subsequent email cannot be overstated; they served as catalysts for change, driving our mission forward and reinforcing our commitment to social justice.

Hiring Community Members as Front-Line Workers: A Commitment to Support and Compliance with California Labor Laws

As we embark on our contract with DHS-ODR, there is an urgent need to hire members from our community for essential roles such as Licensed Vocational Nurses, Case Managers, Program Managers, and multiple Resident Aide monitors. This initiative not only aims to fill these positions but also provides an opportunity to assist individuals who, like me, are returning citizens facing significant challenges in securing stable employment due to their justice-involved backgrounds.

Empowering Our Community

For years, I have prepared myself for this moment—the chance to uplift those in similar situations. Our first wave of hires will consist of 14 individuals, many of whom have faced homelessness and other hardships. We've worked diligently to equip them with essential skills, such as computer literacy and the use of time and attendance applications. This process has not been without its challenges, especially as I navigate new systems within the County as the CEO of a nonprofit organization.

Navigating California Labor Laws

Operating a nonprofit in California requires a keen understanding of labor laws, which are designed to protect employees extensively. These protections can create a complex environment for employers, making it crucial for us to adopt a mindset of running our nonprofit as efficiently as a for-profit business. This approach not only helps us stay compliant but also ensures that we can sustainably support our employees.

Expanding Our Impact

As we are preparing to launch our first housing unit with 23 beds, I received an exciting call from the County to establish a second location. I enthusiastically agreed and am now organizing training sessions and workshops for the next group of potential hires. Many of our employees have experienced significant struggles, and my motivation lies in helping them regain stability.

Addressing Employee Concerns

However, as we began to integrate these individuals into our workforce, we encountered unexpected challenges. Complaints regarding pay, overtime, and promotions arose, often from those we had extended additional support to, including free housing. Despite our efforts to provide a nurturing environment, these grievances became overwhelming.

In California, labor laws stipulate that terminating an employee can lead to retaliation claims, making it essential for us to handle these situations with care. Even in cases of theft, we found ourselves settling complaints to avoid potential legal repercussions. This experience has been disheartening, yet it has not deterred us from our mission.

Fostering a Positive Workplace Culture

In response to these challenges, we have implemented new levels of training and developed a positive workplace culture. Our commitment to our employees remains steadfast, even when the individuals we help the most express feelings of entitlement. We continue to focus on building a supportive environment where all employees can thrive, reinforcing the idea that our work is about more than just providing jobs—it's about fostering dignity and respect.

As we move forward, we remain dedicated to both our mission of helping returning citizens and our obligation to adhere to California's labor laws, ensuring that we cultivate a workplace that is not only productive but also compassionate and fair.

Not to discourage folks from doing business in California, I just want readers to beware and to set yourself up for success. No amount of success will prevent lawsuits and complaints, I talk to the best of the best leaders in the nonprofit and for-profit world, and they all tell me that they will never go away, so many people are simply looking for a quick fix. When they see someone else's success, they see dollar signs for themselves, so get over it.' This means creative ways to secure funding, funding and revenue that allows you to pay for great attorneys and legal advisors that will at least keep you worry free from being a failed CEO.

WHERE DID I GO WRONG?

Lessons learned, a lot can be said about this chapter, but I will start by saying, I started my journey with incredible odds again me as a formerly incarcerated person with no experience in running a massive business or organization. I did go back to school while I was inside, I was able to advance my Islamic education on a scholarly level, but I only achieved an AA degree in Small Business Management, which was the only access that I had at the time within the Correctional system in the early 2000's. My success has been fueled by raw talent as an entrepreneur and a passion to give back to my community no matter the struggle. I would not give up on my people no matter how many times they stab me in the back, I just try harder to see the knife coming and counter with a different strategy which is the reason I believe Timelist Group is still here after 12+ years at the time of the authoring of this book. We watch so many other nonprofits fail, so many leaders give up, so many with great ideas just do not push through this work, but we must have the successful mindset that great things are not achieved without hardship and struggle. What rests on my mind is a conversation that I had with a mentor of mines in 2019, as I sat in her office for about an hour she told me, well Yusef its amazing how you brought in all these people into your organization with Justice Involved background, because we are just starting to do that. We started by bringing in people with skills who had the letters behind their names before we started bringing in folks with lived experience.' So, where did I go wrong, was this a mistake or did I simply start the building process wrong? Or did I have the resources to build from the top down? I think that I gave opportunities to people that I knew before I was well established and in turn that became entitled to everything under the sun and when I said no, they came after me. I think that I also went wrong by not going back to school initially upon being released from prison to secure a BA in Business Administration. To become a great nonprofit leader, even if you lack formal education, you must embrace a proactive and relentless approach to learning and development. Here are some explicit steps to guide you:

1. Understand the Landscape: Start by thoroughly researching the nonprofit sector. Familiarize yourself with key concepts, such as governance, funding models, and community impact. Resources like books, online courses, and podcasts focused on nonprofit management can provide valuable insights.

2. Learn the Legal Framework: Nonprofits must adhere to specific laws and regulations. Take the time to study the legal

requirements for operating a nonprofit in your area. This includes understanding tax-exempt status, reporting requirements, and compliance issues. Consider attending workshops or webinars hosted by legal experts in nonprofit law.

3. Develop Business Acumen: Recognize that running a nonprofit is akin to running a business. Seek out resources that teach business fundamentals, such as budgeting, strategic planning, and marketing. Online platforms like Coursera or LinkedIn Learning offer courses that can help you develop these essential skills.

4. Build a Strong Network: Surround yourself with experienced nonprofit leaders and professionals who can offer mentorship and guidance. Attend industry conferences, join local nonprofit associations, and participate in networking events to connect with others in the field.

5. Gain Practical Experience: Volunteer or intern with established nonprofits to gain hands-on experience. This will not only enhance your understanding of the sector but also help you build a resume and develop important relationships.

6. Seek Feedback and Reflect: As you navigate your nonprofit journey, actively seek feedback from peers, mentors, and those you serve. Use this feedback to reflect on your leadership style and make necessary adjustments.

7. Embrace Lifelong Learning: Commit to continuous education. Stay updated on trends and challenges in the nonprofit sector by subscribing to relevant publications, joining professional organizations, and participating in ongoing training.

8. Create a Sustainable Vision: Focus on building a nonprofit that can thrive beyond your leadership. This means developing a clear mission, creating robust systems and processes, and fostering a strong board of directors who are invested in the organization's longevity.

By taking these steps, you can transform your lack of formal education into a unique strength, equipping yourself to lead a successful nonprofit organization that is resilient and impactful. Remember, great leaders are not defined by their formal education but by their willingness to learn, adapt, and persevere in the face of challenges. The educational barriers faced by African American communities are multifaceted and deeply entrenched in systemic inequalities. Unfortunately, many of these communities find themselves disconnected from educational opportunities that are not only accessible but also transformative opportunities that can empower individuals to emerge as leaders within their own communities.

One significant barrier is the lack of funding for schools predominantly serving African American students. Many of these schools are under-resourced, with inadequate facilities, outdated textbooks, and limited access to technology. This disparity in funding often leads to larger class sizes and fewer experienced teachers, creating an environment where students are not receiving the quality education they deserve.

Additionally, there are societal challenges that play a critical role. Factors such as poverty, high crime rates, and a lack of community support systems can hinder students' ability to focus on their education. Many students face the dual pressures of navigating their academic responsibilities while also dealing with the stresses of their home environments. This often results in lower academic performance and a diminished sense of self-worth.

Moreover, systemic racism and discrimination further exacerbate these barriers. African American students frequently encounter biases within educational institutions, from disciplinary actions that disproportionately affect them to lower expectations set by educators. This can lead to a cycle of disenfranchisement where students feel alienated and unsupported, diminishing their aspirations for higher education and leadership roles.

The lack of access to advanced coursework, mentorship programs, and extracurricular activities also limits the opportunities for personal and professional growth. Without exposure to diverse career paths and role models, many young African Americans may not envision themselves in leadership positions or may lack the guidance needed to pursue such aspirations.

Furthermore, the cultural relevance of the curriculum is often lacking. Educational materials that do not reflect the histories, contributions, and experiences of African Americans can lead to disengagement and a sense of disconnect from the learning process. When students do not see themselves represented in what they are learning, it can diminish their motivation and pride in their educational journey.

Despite these significant challenges, it is crucial that we remain steadfast in our commitment to the African American community. We cannot afford to give up; instead, we must strive to dismantle these barriers. This requires a collective effort to advocate for equitable funding, culturally responsive teaching, and community engagement initiatives that uplift and empower African American students. By working together, we can help cultivate a generation of leaders who are not only educated but also equipped to drive change within our communities across America and the world.

WHAT DID I DO RIGHT?

The first point to be made here is that I've stayed committed to my Faith (Islam), I forgive everyone, I hold no grudges and no judgement. I stayed married, I reconnected with my family and children from my former marriage prior to my incarceration and I remain clean and sober. I never stop reading books the way I did when I was in prison, probably not at the same level but I did not stop. I continue to love people in my community, I don't think that we can solve problems by holding grudges, not having a heart of forgiveness, we must forgive people and move on. As for business, I realized that I needed experts on the team, I could continue as the sole leader with all the answers and solutions, that was very unwise of me. So, the organization grew to a multimillion-dollar operating budget. It allowed me to hire lawyers, bring HR specialists, hire a CPA firm and hire grant writers and fund development officers. As I'm doing this, I'm able to pull myself more out of the day-to-day operations which allow me to work more on big picture operations, running the business from the outside instead of the inside. As 2020 hit, you know what that means ... It's COVID PANDEMIC TIME! I was a bit worried initially, but later we learned that we would get county support to stay in operations during this difficult time. Now here comes inflation, because of COVID many operations across the globe turned to our little friend called ZOOM, Google Meet or Microsoft Teams, this allowed me to host workshops online both for my nonprofit as well as my consultant firm that was gaining more traction over the years. Now I have a platform to serve my Timelist Team and my Consultancy clients. I even started a few online stores during Covid, that entrepreneurship was hard at work as staying vaccinated and travelling with my masks. Coming gradually out of COVID we managed to secure several important State grants, additional contracts with the county and we grew to about 130 employees by July 2022. All money isn't good money which I learned would mean that I should scale back down to quality, not quantity. I believe that I made more enemies during these years, but I could not sacrifice my self-care, sanity and peace of mind. Now I know what my dad meant when he always says, "You pay the cost to be the boss.'

I will now take this moment to acknowledge my parents as they passed away after the pandemic year, but I thank Allah, that I was able to spend the 10 years that I had with them on earth. These were the hardest and most humbling years of my life after prison.

During those long, reflective hours, I discovered something profound—I was becoming more like my parents than I ever imagined. Their unwavering presence during my years of incarceration was a lifeline, and through it all, my father and I forged an unbreakable bond, transforming from mere family into the best of friends. Their love and sacrifices will forever leave an indelible mark on my soul and on the hearts of our entire family, shaping us in ways that will echo through generations.

The foundation of my successis built upon a set of deeply held values that transcend mere quantitative measures. These principles serve as my guiding compass, helping me navigate the complexities of life and decision-making on a profound metaphysical level. Here's a detailed exploration of these essential building blocks:

1. Faith as a Driving Force: At the heart of my journey lies an unwavering faith that significantly influences my thoughts, choices, and actions. This faith is not limited to religious beliefs; rather, it encompasses a broader trust in the inherent goodness of life and the universe. It fuels my resilience during challenging times and inspires me to pursue my goals with conviction. By embracing faith, I cultivate a mindset that encourages optimism and a belief in the potential for positive outcomes, both for myself and for those I guide.

2. Sanctity of Marriage: I hold a deep respect for the institution of marriage, viewing it as a cornerstone of a stable and thriving society. This commitment extends beyond romantic partnerships; it encapsulates the values of loyalty, mutual support, and collaboration. I see marriage as a sacred bond that fosters personal growth and community strength. By honoring this institution, I emphasize the importance of strong, healthy relationships as foundational to both individual fulfillment and societal well-being.

3. Respect for All People, Traditions, and Cultures: Embracing diversity is central to my philosophy. I strive to show reverence for the myriad of backgrounds, beliefs, and customs that enrich our world. This respect fosters inclusivity and understanding, allowing me to connect with individuals on a deeper level. By valuing different perspectives, I create an atmosphere where everyone feels acknowledged and appreciated, which is essential for collaboration and collective growth.

4. Belief in Second Chances and Justice: I am a staunch advocate for the idea that everyone deserves a second chance. This belief underscores my commitment to fairness and equality, as I recognize that growth often comes from overcoming adversity. I support individuals in their journeys, providing them with opportunities to learn from their mistakes and evolve. By promoting a sense of justice, I help create a more equitable society where each person can thrive and contribute positively.

5. Importance of Discipline: Discipline is a crucial element in the pursuit of dreams and aspirations. I firmly believe that without it, progress can be stunted. Discipline involves not only self-control but also the dedication to consistently work towards one's goals. By instilling the value of discipline in myself and others, I emphasize the importance of commitment, resilience, and the capacity to navigate challenges. This principle serves as a reminder that success is often the result of persistent effort and unwavering focus.

These values are more than mere principles; they are the essence of my identity as a CEO, consultant, and speaker. They reflect my commitment to integrity, empathy, inclusivity, and perseverance. By embodying these ideals, I strive to guide and support others on their journeys, empowering them to realize their potential and contribute meaningfully to their communities.

THE SPECTRUM

UNDERSTANDING AUTISM SPECTRUM DISORDER: A PERSONAL JOURNEY

Autism Spectrum Disorder (ASD) is a complex neurodevelopmental condition that affects how individuals perceive the world and interact with others. It encompasses a wide range of behaviors and challenges, leading to the term "spectrum," which acknowledges the diverse experiences of those affected. For some, the impact is mild, while for others, it can be profound and life-altering. The journey of understanding ASD often begins with a personal story, one that reflects the emotional landscape of families navigating this path.

I would later come to learn the meaning of the Spectrum and what Autism truly is. It started with a gnawing feeling that something was off about my son, Amir. As parents, my wife and I noticed that Amir wasn't like the average kid growing up. There were subtle signs at first—delays in his ability to learn and communicate. I remember those early moments when he would walk on his tiptoes, seemingly lost in a world of his own, and would flick the light switches, entranced by the flickering glow.

His diet shifted dramatically, transforming from a variety of foods like eggs and green peas to a singular obsession with French fries from fast-food chains like McDonald's and Carl's Jr. It felt as though we had lost control; we could no longer persuade him to try anything else or even drink water, as he insisted on only consuming a specific type of juice.

After weeks of unease, I finally convinced my wife that something wasn't right. We reached out to friends in the Bay Area—people with expertise in developmental disorders. They asked probing questions about Amir's behavior and, after long, heartfelt conversations, urged us to seek professional help. Though we were still grappling with denial, deep down, I knew we needed to take him to a doctor.

As fate would have it, Amir had an annual check-up scheduled. When we arrived, his pediatrician immediately noticed his tendency to walk on his toes. The moment we exchanged worried glances, an unspoken understanding settled between us. The physician's concern confirmed our fears, and she recommended a specialist in a different building. I felt a surge of anxiety, knowing that the information we would receive might be difficult to bear.

The day of the appointment arrived, and as we sat in the waiting room, I could feel my heart racing. The doctors observed Amir for about 5-10 minutes before they initiated that heart-wrenching conversation. "Your son is indeed on the spectrum," they said. In that moment, I fought to hold back tears, trying to be strong for my wife, who had broken down.

Once we reached our car, the dam burst. I cried, overwhelmed by a mix of sorrow and determination. I looked at my wife and said, "We got this, babe. We are going to get him all of the care that he needs." Amir was just three years old when he received his diagnosis, and it felt like our world had been turned upside down.

As we began to process this new reality, I found myself grappling with many questions. What causes autism? Why are so many parents facing similar challenges today? Theories abound —some point fingers at milk formulas, while others blame vaccination cocktails. Amir had missed a few vaccinations, but when we took him to a clinic in Newark, California, he received a cocktail of shots. It was shortly after this visit that we began to notice the significant changes in his behavior.

What struck me was how many other parents shared the same story. At Autism Speaks walks and in online chat rooms, I encountered countless families recounting identical experiences. This shared narrative brought a strange sense of comfort, yet it also left us with lingering questions.

Ultimately, who really knows what causes autism? All I know is that I continue to pray to Allah for Amir. I pray that one day, he will find his voice and speak to us in a way that we can understand. Until then, we remain committed to providing him with the love, support, and resources he needs to thrive on his unique journey through life. Our immediate family has been incredibly supportive as we navigate this challenging time together. I am especially grateful for our older children, who have shown remarkable kindness and patience towards their little brother. They have embraced their role with such grace and compassion, always finding ways to engage with him and provide comfort. It truly warms my heart to witness their bond and the special moments they share. I often find myself tearing up when I reflect on how fortunate we are to have such a loving and understanding family. Their unwavering support and love have made all the difference, and I cherish each day we spend together, knowing that we are in this as a united front.

If you are a new parent, that might suspect that your child is gifted in a different way. Here are 10 tips for parents who are learning that their child might be on the autism spectrum:

1. Educate Yourself: Learn about autism spectrum disorder (ASD) to better understand your child's behaviors, strengths, and challenges. Books, reputable websites, and local support groups can be valuable resources.

2. Seek Professional Guidance: Consult with healthcare professionals, such as pediatricians, psychologists, or developmental specialists, who can provide accurate assessments and recommendations for interventions.

3. Connect with Support Networks: Join support groups for parents of children with autism. Sharing experiences with others can provide emotional support and practical advice.

4. Focus on Strengths: Every child has unique strengths. Cele-

brate and nurture these abilities, whether they are in academics, arts, or social skills.

5. Create a Structured Environment: Many children on the spectrum thrive in structured settings. Establish routines and clear expectations to help your child feel secure and understand what is coming next.

6. Communicate Clearly: Use clear, concise language when communicating with your child. Visual aids, social stories, and other communication tools can also be helpful.

7. Encourage Social Skills: Facilitate opportunities for your child to interact with peers in a safe and supportive environment. Structured playdates or social skills groups can be beneficial.

8. Practice Self-Care: Caring for a child with autism can be demanding. Make time for your own mental and physical well-being to ensure you can be the best advocate and support for your child.

9. Be Patient and Flexible: Understand that progress may take time. Be patient with your child and yourself as you navigate this journey together.

10. Advocate for Your Child: Learn about your child's rights in education and healthcare. Be proactive in communicating with teachers, therapists, and other professionals to ensure your child receives the support they need.

These tips aim to empower parents as they navigate the challenges and joys of raising a child on the autism spectrum.

FOLLOW THESE STEPS TO TRUE FREEDOM

10 Steps to Freedom: A Comprehensive Guide.

Achieving personal freedom—both financially and emotionally—requires a multi-faceted approach. Here, we will explore ten essential steps that can help you create a life of security, purpose, and continual growth. Each step is designed to protect you and your family from harm, foster personal development, and ensure long-term financial stability.

Step 1: Set Life Goals that Protect You and Your Family from Mental and Physical Harm

Defining Your Goals

Setting life goals is the cornerstone of a fulfilling life. These goals should focus on your well-being and that of your loved ones. Begin by reflecting on what matters most to you. Consider your values, passions, and the legacy you want to leave behind.

Strategies for Goal Setting

1. SMART Goals: Ensure your goals are Specific, Measurable, Achievable, Relevant, and Time-bound.

- Specific: Clearly define what you want to achieve.
- Measurable: Establish criteria to measure your progress.
- Achievable: Set realistic goals that are attainable.
- Relevant: Align your goals with your values and long-term vision.
- Time-bound: Set deadlines to create urgency.

2. Visualization: Imagine your ideal life and the steps needed to achieve it. Visualization can be a powerful motivator.

3. Write It Down: Document your goals. Writing them down not only clarifies your intentions but also serves as a commitment to action.

Protecting Mental and Physical Well-being

When setting goals, prioritize mental and physical health. This includes:

- Work-Life Balance: Aim to create a balance that allows for relaxation and family time.
- Healthy Lifestyle Choices: Include goals for fitness, nutrition, and mental health practices like mindfulness or therapy.
- Emergency Planning: Develop a safety plan for

emergencies, including financial, health, and personal safety measures.

Step 2: Find a Cause or Causes That You Will Support or Create Your Own Nonprofit

The Importance of Giving Back

Supporting a cause that resonates with you can provide a sense of purpose and fulfillment. It can also create a positive impact on your community and beyond.

Steps to Identify Your Cause

1. Reflect on Your Values: What issues are you passionate about? Consider areas such as education, environment, health, or social justice.

2. Research Organizations: Look for nonprofits that align with your values. Attend their events or volunteer to get a feel for their mission.

3. Consider Starting Your Own Nonprofit: If you have a unique vision, consider creating a nonprofit organization.

Impact of Philanthropy

- Community Engagement: Involvement in causes fosters a sense of community and belonging.
- Skill Development: Volunteering can enhance your skills and expand your network.
- Emotional Well-being: Helping others can boost your mood and overall mental health.

Step 3: Make a Monthly Budget

Understanding the Importance of Budgeting

Creating a budget is crucial for achieving financial freedom. It helps you track income and expenses, ensuring that you live within your means and save for future goals.

Steps to Create a Budget

1. Track Your Income: List all sources of income, including salary, side hustles, and investments.

2. List Fixed and Variable Expenses:

- Fixed Expenses: Rent/mortgage, insurance, subscriptions.
- Variable Expenses: Groceries, entertainment, dining out.

3. Set Savings Goals: Allocate a portion of your income to savings and investments.

4. Review and Adjust: Regularly revisit your budget to make adjustments as needed.

Tools for Budgeting

Consider using budgeting tools or apps that can help you track and visualize your finances more effectively.

Step 4: Don't Allow Yourself to Fall into Credit Card or Loan Debts, Pay Off in Full

The Dangers of Debt

Debt can be a significant barrier to financial freedom. High-interest rates can lead to a cycle of borrowing that is hard to escape.

Strategies to Avoid Debt

1. Live Within Your Means: Stick to your budget and avoid lifestyle inflation.

2. Use Cash or Debit Cards: Reduce the temptation to overspend by using cash or debit rather than credit.

3. Plan for Purchases: Save for big purchases instead of relying on credit.

Paying Off Existing Debt

If you do have debt, prioritize paying it off:

- Create a Debt Repayment Plan: Use methods like the snowball or avalanche method to tackle debts systematically.
- Negotiate with Creditors: Don't hesitate to discuss payment plans with creditors if you're struggling.

Step 5: Create Automatic Savings

The Power of Automatic Savings

In today's fast-paced world, managing finances can often feel overwhelming. The constant juggling of bills, expenses, and savings goals can lead to anxiety and, at times, neglecting the essential practice of saving. This is where the power of automatic savings comes into play, transforming the way individuals approach their financial health.

What is Automatic Savings?

Automatic savings is a financial strategy where a predetermined amount of money is automatically transferred from your checking account to a savings account at regular intervals. This can be set up through your bank or financial institution, and it can occur weekly, bi-weekly, or monthly. The beauty of this system lies in its simplicity and efficiency, allowing individuals to save without having to remember to do so actively.

Benefits of Automatic Savings

1. Consistency and Discipline: One of the most significant advantages of automatic savings is the consistency it promotes. By automatically setting aside money, you create a disciplined saving habit. This reduces the temptation to spend that money on immediate wants or needs.

2. Reaching Financial Goals: Whether you're saving for a vacation, a new car, or a home down payment, automatic savings can help you reach those goals faster. By contributing a set amount regularly, you can watch your savings grow, making those dreams a reality.

3. Reduced Stress: Knowing that your savings are being handled automatically can alleviate financial stress. You won't have to worry about whether you remembered to save each month,

allowing you to focus on other financial responsibilities.

4. Building an Emergency Fund: Having an emergency fund is crucial for financial stability. Automatic savings can help you build this fund over time, ensuring that you are prepared for unexpected expenses without derailing your budget.

5. Investment Opportunities: Some individuals choose to automate their savings into investment accounts. This can lead to potential growth through compound interest, making your savings work harder for you over time.

6. Encouraging Smart Spending: When you automate your savings, you often have a clearer picture of your disposable income. This can encourage smarter spending habits, as you'll be more aware of how much money you actually have left after savings.

How to Set Up Automatic Savings

1. Choose Your Savings Goal: Determine what you are saving for. This could be a short-term goal, like a vacation, or a long-term goal, like retirement.

2. Decide on the Amount: Assess your budget and decide how much you can afford to save each month without impacting on your essential expenses.

3. Select the Right Account: Choose a high-yield savings account or an investment account that aligns with your goals. Look for accounts with low fees and favorable interest rates.

4. Set Up Automatic Transfers: Use your bank's online banking

system to set up automatic transfers. Specify the amount and frequency of the transfers to ensure they align with your pay schedule.

5. Monitor Your Progress: Regularly check your savings account to monitor your progress. Adjust the amount or frequency of transfers as necessary to stay on track with your goals.

* * *

Automatic savings is a powerful tool in personal finance that can help individuals achieve their financial goals with minimal effort. By leveraging the power of automation, you can cultivate consistent saving habits, reduce financial stress, and turn aspirations into reality. Whether you're saving for a large purchase or building an emergency fund, setting up automatic savings can put you on the path to financial security and peace of mind. Take the first step today and experience the transformative effects of automatic savings in your financial journey.

For me, after learning so much from studying and reading I realized that the education that I received as a child was not preparing me for the real world that I would soon face. How much are we investing in the financial literacy of our children? Teaching financial education to black and brown kids is essential in today's world, where financial literacy is not just a beneficial skill but a necessity for navigating life's complexities. The education system often falls short in equipping students with the knowledge they need to manage their finances effectively, particularly in minority communities where socioeconomic challenges are prevalent. Reflecting on my own experiences, I realize that the education I received did not prepare me for the realities of adult life, especially in terms of financial management. This gap in financial education is concerning, especially when considering how it affects minority children who are already facing systemic barriers.

The investment in financial literacy education for children varies widely across different communities, and public schools often struggle to provide comprehensive financial education. The curriculum in many public schools does not adequately cover essential topics such as budgeting, saving, investing, and understanding credit. As a result, many students graduate without a clear understanding of what money is and how to manage it effectively. This deficiency can have lasting effects, particularly for minority students who may not have access to resources or mentorship outside of school that could help them fill these gaps.

The lack of financial education can perpetuate cycles of poverty within minority communities. When children grow up without understanding how to manage money, they are more likely to make financial mistakes that can lead to debt and financial instability. This instability can further limit their opportunities for higher education, homeownership, and overall financial security. Financial literacy serves as a foundation for making informed decisions that can lead to economic empowerment. Teaching minority kids about money management can provide them with the tools they need to break free from the constraints of their socioeconomic status.

Empowerment through financial knowledge is a crucial aspect of teaching financial education. When children learn about budgeting and saving, they gain confidence in their ability to manage their financial futures. This empowerment can lead to greater participation in higher education and entrepreneurship, as financially literate individuals are more likely to take calculated risks, invest in their education, or start their own businesses. The ability to understand financial concepts allows them to navigate opportunities that might otherwise be inaccessible.

Moreover, financial education contributes to building resilience among minority children. Understanding how to manage money can help them develop coping strategies for financial setbacks. For example, knowing how to create a budget can help students prioritize their spending, allowing them to weather unexpected expenses without falling into debt. This resilience is especially important in communities where economic volatility is common. Children who are equipped with financial knowledge are better prepared to face the challenges of adulthood, leading to more stable and secure lives.

The integration of financial education into school curriculums is essential for addressing these gaps. Schools must prioritize financial literacy as a core subject, just like math or science. This integration can be achieved through partnerships with financial institutions and organizations that specialize in financial education. By providing resources, training, and materials, these partnerships can help educators deliver impactful financial literacy programs that resonate with students. Schools can also incorporate real-life scenarios and practical exercises that engage students and illustrate the importance of financial management.

Community initiatives also play a vital role in enhancing financial literacy among minority children. After-school programs, workshops, and summer camps focused on financial education can provide practical learning experiences that complement what students learn in school. These initiatives can create a supportive environment where children can ask questions and learn from professionals in the financial sector. Mentorship programs can connect students with financial experts who can offer guidance and share their own experiences, making financial concepts more relatable and actionable.

Parents and guardians also have a crucial role in teaching financial literacy. Open discussions about money, budgeting, and saving can reinforce the lessons learned in school. Parents can share their own financial experiences, both successes and mistakes, providing valuable context for their children. Encouraging kids to participate in family budgeting discussions or to set savings goals can make financial education a collaborative effort. Schools and community organizations can support parents by offering resources and workshops that equip them to teach their children about money management.

The broader implications of investing in financial literacy education are significant. Economic empowerment is one of the most important outcomes of teaching financial education to minority kids. As these children grow into financially literate adults, they can contribute to the economic vitality of their communities. Higher levels of financial literacy can lead to increased savings, better credit scores, and a greater likelihood of homeownership. These factors contribute not only to individual financial well-being but also to the overall economic health of communities, creating a positive feedback loop that benefits everyone.

Furthermore, financial education is a matter of social justice and equity. By providing equal access to financial literacy resources, we can help level the playing field for minority children who have historically been marginalized. Financial literacy empowers individuals to advocate for themselves and their communities, promoting equity and opportunity. In a society where financial knowledge often translates to power, ensuring that all children have access to this education is a step toward dismantling systemic barriers.

The current state of financial education in public schools reflects a broader societal issue: the need to recognize and address the disparities that exist in educational resources. Many schools serving minority populations are underfunded and lack the resources necessary to provide comprehensive financial education. This inequity must be addressed

A MESSAGE TO AFRICAN AMERICAN READERS

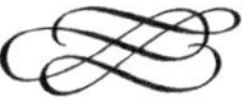

When I went to prison in February 1991, I was sent to a facility that had an orientation intake process requiring me to take what was called a T.A.B.E. (Test of Adult Basic Education). When I took this test, I was scored at a 4th-grade level. Why am I sharing this? Well, I was a gang member when I entered the correctional system. How did I become a gang member, and why? Part of it was the result of struggling in education as a youth, combined with the embarrassment of asking for help and the fear of peer teasing. Consequently, I aligned myself with the youth who refused to turn in homework, acted as class clowns, ditched school, and engaged in marijuana use and alcohol consumption as an escape from educational accountability. This was coupled with a failed public educational system that is underfunded in Black and brown communities.

For an African Americans whose ancestor's-built America and who comes from a rich history of power and culture, this situation was all by design, meant to keep us at the bottom of the barrel as a people. The legacy of slavery and the treatment of African Americans as mere slaves served to keep us from recognizing the richness of our culture, mentally placing us in an underclass. This was a setup from the beginning, preparing us for the school-to-prison pipeline. Black men are disproportionately represented in the prison system, and this troubling trend can be attributed, in part, as stated before, to a complex web of systemic issues within the educational framework, particularly in communities predominantly inhabited by Black individuals. One major factor contributing to this disparity is the chronic underfunding of schools in these areas. Many predominantly Black neighborhoods face significant financial challenges, which directly impact the quality of education available to their residents. Schools in these communities often operate with limited resources, leading to overcrowded classrooms, outdated textbooks, insufficient access to technology, and a lack of extracurricular programs that are essential for holistic development.

The consequences of this inadequate funding are severe. Students in underfunded schools tend to experience lower academic performance, which can manifest in lower graduation rates and diminished opportunities for higher education. This educational disparity not only undermines the potential of young Black men but also limits their access to stable, well-paying jobs in the future. The job market increasingly demands skilled workers with a solid educational background, and without the necessary credentials, many young Black men find themselves unable to compete for these roles. This lack of access to meaningful employment creates a precarious situation where individuals may feel pushed toward illegal activities as a means of financial survival.

In addition to underfunding, the phenomenon known as the school-to-prison pipeline plays a critical role in perpetuating the cycle of disadvantage faced by Black students. This term refers to the policies and practices within educational systems that disproportionately push at-risk students, particularly those from minority backgrounds, out of schools and into the criminal justice system. Many schools implement harsh disciplinary measures, including suspensions and expulsions, often as part of zero-tolerance policies that do not consider the context or circumstances surrounding a student's behavior. Such punitive measures can alienate students from the educational environment, leading to increased absenteeism and, ultimately, dropping out of school.

The impact of these disciplinary practices is profound. When students are removed from their educational settings, they lose critical learning opportunities and are often left without the support systems necessary to guide them toward success. This disconnection from education can lead to feelings of hopelessness and frustration, prompting some individuals to engage in criminal behavior as a way to cope with their circumstances. The intersection of inadequate education and punitive school policies creates a perfect storm that funnels young Black men into the criminal justice system, where they may face further marginalization and stigma.

Moreover, the cycle of limited educational opportunities and increased incarceration perpetuates racial disparities in prison populations. The overrepresentation of Black men in prisons can be traced back to these systemic inequalities that begin in childhood and continue throughout their lives. As many young Black men are funneled into the criminal justice system, they face a myriad of challenges, including legal repercussions, social stigma, and limited access to resources that could help them reintegrate into society.

The repercussions of this cycle extend beyond the individual, affecting entire communities. Families are often torn apart when a member is incarcerated, leading to further economic instability and emotional distress. The cumulative effect of these systemic issues reinforces a narrative of hopelessness and despair, making it increasingly difficult for communities to thrive.

In conclusion, the systemic issues within education and the school-to-prison pipeline create a vicious cycle that disproportionately affects Black men, leading to their overrepresentation in the prison system. Addressing these disparities requires a comprehensive approach that includes increased funding for schools in predominantly Black communities, the implementation of restorative justice practices in educational settings, and a commitment to dismantling the policies that perpetuate this cycle of disadvantages. Only through systemic change can we hope to break the cycle of limited educational opportunities and excessive incarceration, fostering an environment where all individuals, regardless of their background, have the chance to succeed.

This is why prioritizing quality education must be at the forefront of all our efforts within faith communities, households, and society as a whole. Education is not merely a tool for personal advancement; it is the foundation upon which we build a better future for ourselves and our communities. By investing in quality education, we empower individuals to reach their full potential and contribute meaningfully to society. We cannot afford to overlook the immense value of education, as it shapes our understanding, fosters critical thinking, and cultivates the skills necessary for navigating an increasingly complex world. In nurturing an educated populace, we create a more informed and engaged citizenry, capable of addressing the challenges we face together.

GROWTH MINDSET

This has been my mantra in the last 10 years, Growth mindset. What does this even mean? A growth mindset is the belief that abilities and intelligence can be developed through effort and learning. Key traits include:

1. Embracing Challenges: Viewing them as growth opportunities.

2. Persistence: Staying resilient in setbacks.

3. Learning from Criticism: Using feedback to improve.

4. Inspiration from Others: Being motivated by others' success.

5. Focus on Learning: Valuing the learning process over just results.

Overall, it fosters motivation, achievement, and a positive approach to challenges.

Here are more detailed explanations of each growth mindset example:

Embrace New Challenges

Individuals with a growth mindset actively seek out new challenges rather than avoiding them. For instance, someone might take on a difficult project at work that pushes their skills. They view challenges as opportunities for growth, knowing that overcoming obstacles will enhance their capabilities and resilience.

Are Persistent and Don't Give Up

Persistence is a hallmark of a growth mindset. For example, when faced with a setback, such as failing an exam or not getting a promotion, a person with a growth mindset analyzes what went wrong, seeks feedback, and develops a plan to improve. They don't see failure as a reflection of their abilities but rather as a stepping stone toward success.

Practice Self-Care

Practicing self-care is crucial for maintaining a growth mindset. This might involve setting aside time for relaxation, exercise, and hobbies that promote well-being. By prioritizing their mental and physical health, these individuals create a solid foundation that allows them to tackle challenges with a clear mind and renewed energy.

Are Always Learning New Skills

Those with a growth mindset have an insatiable curiosity and commitment to lifelong learning. They might enroll in online courses, attend workshops, or read books to acquire new skills outside their comfort zone. For instance, a professional might learn a new programming language or take up public speaking to enhance their career prospects.

Focus on the Journey, as Well as the Destination

People with a growth mindset appreciate the process of learning and personal development, not just the end result. They celebrate small victories along the way and reflect on the lessons learned from experiences. For example, someone might enjoy the process of preparing for a marathon rather than solely fixating on the race day.

Are Inspired by Others

A growth mindset involves finding inspiration in the success of others. Instead of feeling threatened by someone else's achievements, these individuals celebrate them and use them as motivation to push themselves further. For instance, they might follow a mentor or role model's journey and adopt strategies that resonate with their own goals.

Encourage Others

Encouraging others is a key trait of those with a growth mindset. They uplift peers by providing support and constructive feedback. For example, a teacher might foster a growth-oriented classroom by praising effort over results, thereby inspiring students to take risks and learn from their mistakes.

These examples illustrate how a growth mindset can profoundly influence personal development and relationships, leading to a more fulfilling and successful life.

You must love the learning process.

Four Foundational Principles to consider.

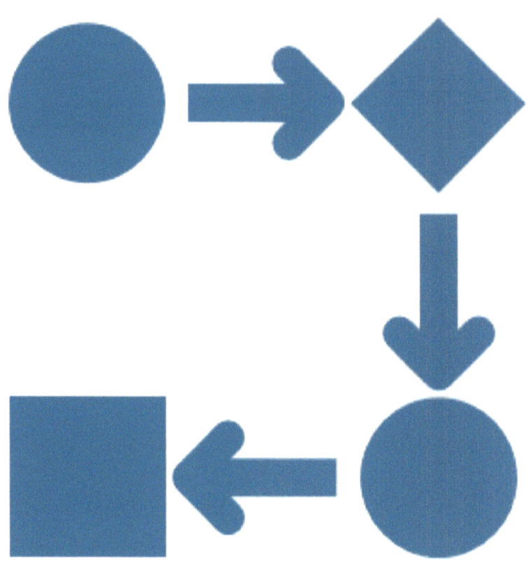

- Faith-Spirituality and/or Mindfulness
- Family, Kinship Bonds
- Career, Workflow
- Diet & Exercise

I Can and I will, no excuses

The Elixir of Transformation: Understanding Discipline

What is Elixir? In the quest for personal and professional growth, the term "elixir" often symbolizes a transformative force —something that can catalyze significant change within us. This elixir is not a physical substance but rather a metaphor for a powerful principle that can lead to profound outcomes.

The Substance That Turns Hard Metals into Gold

In the realm of alchemy, the idea of transforming base metals into gold represents the ultimate achievement of turning something ordinary into something extraordinary. In a similar vein, the substance that facilitates this transformation in our lives is **discipline**.

The Role of Discipline

Discipline acts as the guiding force that enables individuals to hone their skills, maintain focus, and persist through challenges. It is the consistent practice of self-control and dedication that allows one to pursue their goals and realize their potential.

The Four Foundational Principles

To achieve success in any endeavor, it is essential to incorporate the Four Foundational Principles:

1. Clarity of Purpose: Knowing what you want to achieve.

2. Consistent Action: Taking regular steps towards your goals.

3. Resilience: Overcoming obstacles and setbacks.

4. Continuous Learning: Adapting and growing from experience.

However, none of these principles can be effectively realized without the backbone of [discipline]. It is the commitment to uphold these principles that ultimately lead to transformation and success.

In summary, the elixir that transforms the ordinary into the extraordinary is discipline. By embodying this principle, you can harness the power to achieve the Four Foundational Principles and unlock your fullest potential.

Diet and exercise play crucial roles in overall health and well-being, particularly within this context. Here's an explanation of their importance:

1. Stress Reduction: A wholesome diet helps regulate hormones and neurotransmitters that affect mood. Regular exercise promotes the release of endorphins, which are natural stress relievers. Together, they help mitigate stress levels.

2. Energy Levels: A balanced diet provides the essential nutrients and energy needed for daily activities. When you consume foods high in sugars and unhealthy fats, you may experience energy crashes. Regular exercise boosts stamina and combats fatigue, enhancing your overall energy levels.

3. Motivation and Productivity: Poor nutrition and lack of physical activity can lead to feelings of laziness and lethargy. On the other hand, a nutritious diet and regular exercise can enhance motivation, enabling you to stay focused and productive throughout the day.

4. Cognitive Function: Studies suggest that a healthy diet supports brain health, improving memory and concentration. Exercise also increases blood flow to the brain, enhancing

cognitive functions and the ability to concentrate for extended periods.

5. Preventing Health Problems: A balanced diet and regular exercise are vital for maintaining a healthy weight, reducing the risk of chronic diseases such as heart disease, diabetes, and obesity. These health issues can further contribute to stress and fatigue.

Tips for Implementation:

- Drink Plenty of Water: Staying hydrated is essential for optimal body function and helps maintain energy levels.
- Balanced Diet: Focus on whole foods, including fruits, vegetables, lean proteins, and whole grains. Limit red meat and sugary foods to avoid spikes in energy followed by crashes.
- Exercise Regularly: Aim for at least three workouts per week, incorporating both cardio and strength training.
- Daily Walks: Simple activities like walking can improve cardiovascular health and mental well-being.

Self-Assessment:

To gauge your discipline level in achieving these goals, rate yourself on a scale from 0 to 5, where 0 indicates no discipline and 5 indicates complete discipline. Where do you stand?

This self-assessment can help you identify areas for improvement and motivate you to enhance your diet and exercise habits.

AFTERWORD

I would be remiss if I didn't mention the impact of the pandemic. The end of the COVID-19 highlights the profound challenges that arose during this period. Numerous studies identified significant issues, including the limitations on direct human interaction, restrictions on mobility and travel, shifts in lifestyle that reduced physical activity, pervasive feelings of boredom and monotony, and a pervasive uncertainty about what the future holds.

On one side of this spectrum, there was a noticeable decline in the desire for employment, particularly in communities hit hard by the pandemic. This decline led to increased reliance on government stimulus programs, which, in turn, fostered a rise in scams and petty crimes, including theft and burglary. Conversely, the other side of the spectrum saw a surge in entrepreneurship and philanthropic efforts, as individuals sought new avenues for income and ways to support their communities.

Amidst these shifts, there was also a troubling erosion of respect for elders and a decline in traditional faith practices. This raises intriguing questions about the human experience during this time—how can we witness a fall in spirituality while simultaneously seeing the rise of new-age faith traditions and the establishment of new churches and congregations? This paradox reflects the complex nature of human resilience and adaptation in the face of unprecedented challenges.

* * *

During times of pandemics, including the recent COVID-19 outbreak, two key principles have consistently surfaced in both academic and public discussions. These principles have played a crucial role in shaping the psychological responses of individuals and communities within Muslim societies as they navigate the challenges posed by such health crises.

The first principle revolves around the concept of communal solidarity. In the face of widespread illness and uncertainty, Muslim communities often emphasize the importance of collective support and mutual aid. This principle fosters a sense of unity, encouraging individuals to come together to aid those affected by the pandemic. Whether through organized efforts to deliver food and medical supplies, or through emotional support networks, the focus on solidarity helps to alleviate feelings of isolation and fear that can accompany a health crisis.

The second principle relates to the interpretation of illness and suffering through a spiritual lens. In many Muslim societies, pandemics are often viewed not merely as physical afflictions but also as tests of faith and opportunities for spiritual growth. This perspective can significantly shape how individuals cope with the psychological stress associated with disease. Faith-based practices, such as prayer and community gatherings (when safe), can provide comfort and a sense of purpose during tumultuous times. The belief that hardship can lead to spiritual rewards may help individuals maintain hope and resilience in the face of adversity.

Together, these principles of communal solidarity and spiritual interpretation create a framework through which Muslims respond to the psychological impacts of pandemics. They underscore the importance of community ties and faith in navigating the complexities of illness, ultimately influencing both individual behaviors and broader societal responses to public health challenges.

It was a punishment sent by Allah on whom He wished, and Allah made it a source of mercy for the believers, for if at the time of a plague epidemic one stays in his country patiently hoping for Allah's Reward, and believing that nothing will befall him except what Allah has written for him, he will get a reward similar to that of a martyr (Bukhārī, 1997, p. 427).

So, even for the Christians and similar traditions, the themes of faith, patience, and divine will, which can be compared to several biblical passages that convey similar messages.

One relevant biblical quote is from the book of James in the New Testament:

James 1:2-4 (NIV): "Consider it pure joy, my brothers and sisters, whenever you face trials of many kinds, because you know that the testing of your faith produces perseverance. Let perseverance finish its work so that you may be mature and complete, not lacking anything."

Both quotes emphasize the importance of enduring hardship with faith and the belief that such trials can lead to spiritual growth and rewards.

In the Islamic quote, patience during a plague is framed as a path to receiving a divine reward, akin to martyrdom, which aligns with the biblical idea that enduring trials can strengthen one's faith and lead to spiritual maturity.

Thus, both quotes encourage believers to maintain their faith in the face of adversity, trusting in a higher purpose and eventual reward.

CONCLUSION

THE POWER OF FOCUS, PERSEVERANCE, AND INTEGRITY

In the journey of life, we often encounter a myriad of challenges, distractions, and temptations that can sway us from our chosen path. Yet, amidst this chaos, the importance of staying focused, persevering in the pursuit of our dreams, and holding steadfast to the principles that shape our character cannot be overstated. These elements work together to forge not only our personal success but also our development as compassionate, resilient individuals who contribute positively to the world around us.

Staying Focused: The Art of Concentration

Focus is the cornerstone of any successful endeavor. In an age dominated by digital distractions, maintaining concentration has become increasingly difficult. However, the ability to concentrate on our goals is what distinguishes those who succeed from those who falter. Focus allows us to channel our energy and resources toward achieving our dreams, whether they be personal, professional, or creative.

To illustrate, consider the story of renowned author J.K. Rowling, who faced numerous rejections before her Harry Potter series became a global phenomenon. Rowling's unwavering focus on her writing, despite the challenges she faced—unemployment, single parenthood, and financial instability—demonstrates how a clear vision and dedication can yield extraordinary results. By concentrating on her goal and ignoring the naysayers, she not only achieved her dream but also inspired millions around the world.

Moreover, focus requires the ability to prioritize effectively. In a world filled with endless possibilities, it's essential to identify what truly matters. This can involve setting clear, achievable goals and breaking them down into manageable tasks. Such an approach minimizes and enhances productivity. When we prioritize our dreams and eliminate distractions, we create a conducive environment for success.

The Importance of Perseverance

Equally vital is the quality of perseverance. The road to fulfilling our dreams is rarely a straight path; it is often fraught with obstacles and setbacks. However, it is in these moments of difficulty that our true character is revealed. Perseverance is about having the grit to push through adversity, to keep going when the going gets tough, and to refuse to let failures define us.

Thomas Edison, the inventor of the light bulb, famously said, "I have not failed. I've just found 10,000 ways that won't work." His relentless pursuit of innovation exemplifies the spirit of perseverance. Despite numerous failures, he remained committed to his vision, ultimately leading to breakthroughs that changed the world. Edison's story serves as a powerful reminder that the path to success is often littered with failures, but each failure is an opportunity to learn and grow stronger.

Perseverance is also about resilience, the ability to bounce back from setbacks. Life will inevitably throw curveballs in our way, and how we respond defines our trajectory. By embracing challenges and viewing them as opportunities for growth, we cultivate a mindset that empowers us to keep moving forward, even in the face of adversity. This resilience not only helps us achieve our dreams but also builds our character, making us more empathetic and understanding individuals.

Holding on to Principles: The Foundation of Integrity

As we pursue our dreams with focus and perseverance, it is crucial to hold on to the principles that define us. Our values—be it honesty, kindness, respect, or integrity—serve as the moral compass guiding our decisions and actions. In a world where it can be tempting to compromise our principles for short-term gains, staying true to our values becomes even more significant.

Integrity is the foundation upon which lasting success is built. When we act in alignment with our principles, we cultivate trust and respect from others. People are naturally drawn to those who are authentic and principled, as they inspire confidence and foster meaningful relationships. For instance, consider the legacy of leaders like Mahatma Gandhi and Martin Luther King

Jr. Their unwavering commitment to non-violence and justice, even in the face of immense personal risk, not only propelled their movements but also left an indelible mark on history.

Moreover, holding on to our principles during challenging times can serve as a source of strength. When faced with tough decisions, reflecting on our core values can provide clarity and guide us toward choices that align with who we are. This alignment not only fosters personal satisfaction but also contributes to a sense of fulfillment, as we know we are living authentically.

The Interconnectedness of Focus, Perseverance, and Principles

The relationship between focus, perseverance, and principles is symbiotic. Focus enables us to identify our dreams and set clear goals. Perseverance fuels our journey, empowering us to overcome obstacles and stay the course. Meanwhile, our principles anchor us, ensuring that our pursuit of success does not come at the expense of our integrity.

The importance of staying focused, not giving up on our dreams, and holding onto our principles cannot be overstated. These elements are not just paths to personal success; they are also foundational to becoming better individuals who positively impact the world. As we navigate the complexities of life, let us remember that our ambitions are often intertwined with our values. By maintaining clarity of purpose and resilience in the face of challenges, we equip ourselves to pursue our goals while remaining true to who we are. This balance fosters not only our own growth but also inspires those around us to strive for excellence.

Moreover, the journey toward achieving our dreams is rarely linear, and it is during the inevitable setbacks that our commitment to our principles is truly tested. Embracing perseverance allows us to learn from failures and adapt rather than succumb to discouragement. As we uphold our values, we contribute to a culture of integrity and determination, setting an example for others to follow. Ultimately, by combining focus, resilience, and principled living, we can create a ripple effect that encourages collective progress and transforms our aspirations into reality, fostering a brighter future for ourselves and the society we inhabit.

ACKNOWLEDGMENTS

I have to end this with acknowledgement of all of the wonderful people who continue to inspire me, motivate me, teach me and push me to always be the best version of myself. In loving memory of my parents Sampson and Betty Wiley, my wife Sanae Wiley, my sisters Donna and Pamela Wiley, my mentors and teachers of the years, Shaykh Rami Nsour and the Nsour family, Babar Raza and his brother Khalid Raza, Imam Michael Salaam, my friends and colleagues, Taahir Prather, Cortez Chandler, Charles Taylor, Khalis Benard Holloway, Ustadh-Tabari Zahir, Amin Rafiq, Imam Jihad Saafir. Please forgive me for not including so many others that I indeed consider to be my friends. And of course, my beautiful children and grandchildren.

Yusef Andre Wiley

www.ingramcontent.com/pod-product-compliance
Lightning Source LLC
LaVergne TN
LVHW021333160826
845679LV00008B/1352

* 9 7 9 8 8 9 5 6 9 9 8 2 9 *